TOOLS OF WAR

WEAPONS and VEHICLES of WORLD WAR I

by Elizabeth Summers

Reading Consultant:
Barbara J. Fox
Professor Emerita
North Carolina State University

CAPS

a c

Blazers Books are published by Capstone Press,
1710 Roe Crest Drive, North Mankato, Minnesota 56003.
www.capstonepub.com

Library of Congress Cataloging-in-Publication Data

Summers, Elizabeth.
Weapons and vehicles of World War I / by Elizabeth Summers.
      pages cm.—(Blazers books. Tools of war)
Includes bibliographical references and index.
Audience: Grades K-3.
ISBN 978-1-4914-4095-7 (library binding)
ISBN 978-1-4914-4117-6 (ebook pdf)
1. World War, 1914-1918—Equipment and supplies—Juvenile literature. 2. Vehicles, Military—
History—20th century—Juvenile literature. 3. World War, 1914-1918—Transportation—Juvenile
literature. I. Title.
D522.7.S87 2016
940.4—dc23   2015009399

Editorial Credits

Anna Butzer, editor; Heidi Thompson, designer; Jo Miller, media researcher;
Katy LaVigne, production specialist

Photo Credits

Alamy: Historic Collection, 5, INTERFOTO, 9 (both); Corbis: Hulton-Deutsch Collection, 25;
Getty Images: SSPL, 7; National Archives and Records Administration, 15, 22; Newscom:
akg-images, cover, 16, 19, 26, 28, ZB/picture alliance/Archiv/Berliner Verlag, 21; Shutterstock:
Gary Blakeley, 13 (bottom), Jeffrey B. Banke, 13 (top); Wikimedia: Armémuseum (The Swedish
Army Museum), 11

Design Elements:
Shutterstock: angelinast, aodaodaodaod, artjazz, Brocreative, ilolab, kasha_malasha, Peter Sobolev

Printed in the United States of America in North Mankato, Minnesota.
052015   008823CGF15

TABLE OF CONTENTS

THE WAR TO END ALL WARS

World War I (1914-1918) began when Austria's Archduke Franz Ferdinand was **assassinated** in 1914. Nations divided into two groups after his murder. On one side were the Central Powers. On the other side were the Allied nations. The United States entered the war in 1917.

assassinate–to murder an important or famous person

Fact

More than 65 million soldiers fought in World War I. The youngest soldier was only 8 years old.

Militaries used several new weapons during World War I. Other weapons and vehicles were not widely used before the war.

Fact

More than 37 million soldiers were killed during World War I. The war was called "The War to End All Wars."

German A7V tank

WEAPONS

Rifles

Rifles and handguns improved during World War I. Many nations used similar rifles. The 1918 German Mauser T-Gewehr was the world's first antitank rifle. It weighed 35 pounds (16 kilograms) and was nicknamed the "elephant gun."

Fact

The Russian Army used the Mosin-Nagant rifle. It was one of the most successful weapons of the war.

Mauser T-Gewehr

Mosin-Nagant Rifle

The rifles used **magazines** and bolt-action loading systems. These rifles kicked out a **shell** and loaded a new one at the same time.

	1903 Springfield	Lebel 1893	
Country	United States	France	
Weight	8.5 pounds (3.8 kg)	9.2 pounds (4.1 kg)	
Length	3.6 feet (1.1 m)	4.3 feet (1.3 m)	
Firing Range	1,000 yards (914 m)	438 yards (400 m)	

magazine—a metal or plastic case that holds bullets and fits inside a gun

shell—a metal or paper case holding the explosive charge and shot or bullet used in light weapons

range—the longest distance at which a weapon can still hit its target

1898 Mauser

	1891 Mosin-Nagant	1898 Mauser	Lee Enfield .303
	Russia	Germany	Great Britain
	9 pounds (4 kg)	9 pounds (4 kg)	8.7 pounds (3.9 kg)
	4.3 feet (1.3 m)	4.1 feet (1.2 m)	3.6 feet (1.1 m)
	550 yards (503 m)	550 yards (503 m)	550 yards (503 m)

Handguns and Knives

Handguns and knives were used as **sidearms**. World War I soldiers used these weapons to defend themselves when fighting at close range. German Lugers were one of the best handguns of the war.

	Webley Mark VI	Steyr Automatic	Luger	Browning-Colt Model 1911
Country	Great Britain	Austria-Hungary, Romania	Germany	United States
Ammunition	.455-caliber bullets	9mm bullets	9mm bullets	.455-caliber bullets
Weight	2.4 pounds (1.1 kg)	2.6 pounds (1.2 kg)	2 pounds (1 kg)	2 pounds (1 kg)
Number of Rounds	6	8	8	7

sidearm—a weapon worn at the side or in the belt

Webley Mark VI

Luger

Soldiers used knives and **bayonets** during close **combat**. Bayonets were popular with German soldiers. Russian soldiers used trooper daggers that were longer than the German bayonet.

Fact

The German bayonet was 10.25 inches (26 cm) long. The Russian trooper dagger blade was more than 17 inches (43 cm) long.

bayonet–a long metal blade attached to the end of a musket or rifle
combat–fighting between people or militaries

bayonet training

Grenades, Trench Clubs, and Flamethrowers

The fighting in **trenches** was very dangerous. Soldiers threw many types of **grenades** into enemy trenches. Soldiers made trench clubs from nails, spikes, and metal rods. Flamethrowers used a mix of oil and gasoline to blast fire at enemies.

flamethrowers

trench–a long, deep area dug into the ground with dirt piled up on one side for defense

grenade–a small bomb that can be thrown or launched

Machine Guns and Heavy Field Guns

Many heavy weapons were used for the first time during World War I. These weapons caused more destruction than ever before. Field guns fired heavy shells at targets several miles away. The Mark I was Britain's largest field gun.

	75mm Field Gun	The British Mark I	42cm Howitzer
Gun Weight	1.3 tons (1 mt)	4 tons (3 mt)	75 tons (68 mt)
Shell Weight	16 pounds (7 kg)	60 pounds (27 kg)	2,052 pounds (930 kg)
Firing Range	4 miles (6 km)	6 miles (9 km)	9 miles (14 km)

howitzer

VEHICLES

Tanks

Great Britain's use of tanks changed the outcome of the war. The first tank **assault** happened in September 1916. Britain's new vehicles surprised the German forces.

Fact

British Mark I tanks came in "male" and "female" versions. They had different types of ammunition.

assault–a violent or sudden attack

Mark IV tank

Several tanks had **turrets** that made them more powerful. The French Renault FT-17 was the first tank with a turret that could turn around in a full circle. This design allowed the tanks weapons to fire in any direction.

	British Mark IV (male)	German A-7	French Schnieder	Renault FT-17
Weapons Carried	two 57mm guns	57mm gun, six heavy machine guns	75mm gun, two Hotchkiss machine guns	37mm gun or Hotchkiss machine gun
Speed	3.5 miles per hour (5 km/hr)	4 miles per hour (6 km/hr)	5 miles per hour (8 km/hr)	5 miles per hour (8 km/hr)

Renault FT-17

turret–a rotating structure on top of a military vehicle that holds a weapon

Ships

Battleships existed long before World War I began. But warships greatly improved in size and firepower during the war. The HMS *Dreadnought* was a very successful British warship. It led the British navy to create a special Dreadnought class of battleships.

	HMS Dreadnought	SMS Nassau	HMS Queen Elizabeth
Country	Britain	Germany	Britain
Weapons Carried	12-inch guns mounted on twin turrets, twenty-four 12-pound guns	twelve 11-inch (28-cm), twelve 5.9-inch (15-cm), and sixteen 3.4-inch (8-cm) guns	eight 15-inch (38-cm) guns, twelve 6-inch (15-cm) guns, and twelve 12-pound guns

HMS Dreadnought

Modern **submarines** were used for the first time during World War I. A German U-19 class submarine sank the famous British passenger ship RMS *Lusitania*.

German submarines

submarine—a ship that can travel both on the surface of and under the water

Planes

Airplanes were widely used for the first time during World War I. Fighter planes were the most common. World War I was a war of great invention as well as terrible destruction.

British fighter planes

Fact

The German **ace** Baron Manfred von Richthofen flew a Fokker DR-1 plane. Richthofen was nicknamed "The Red Baron" because he painted his plane bright red.

ace–a top fighter pilot

GLOSSARY

ace (AYS)—a top fighter pilot

assassinate (us-SASS-uh-nate)—to murder an important or famous person

assault (uh-SAWLT)—a violent or sudden attack

bayonet (BAY-uh-net)—a long metal blade attached to the end of a musket or rifle

combat (KOM-bat)—fighting between people or militaries

grenade (gruh-NAYD)—a small bomb that can be thrown or launched

magazine (MAG-uh-zeen)—a metal or plastic case that holds bullets and fits inside a gun

range (RAYNJ)—the longest distance at which a weapon can still hit its target

shell (SHEL)—a metal or paper case holding the explosive charge and shot or bullet used in light weapons

sidearm (SIHD-ahrm)—a weapon worn at the side or in the belt

submarine (SUHB-muh-reen)—a ship that can travel both on the surface of and under the water

trench (TRENCH)—a long, deep area dug into the ground with dirt piled up on one side for defense

turret (TUR-it)—a rotating structure on top of a military vehicle that holds a weapon

READ MORE

Fein, Eric. *Weapons, Gear, and Uniforms of World War I.* Equipped for Battle. Mankato, Minn.: Capstone Pub., 2012.

Samuels, Charlie. *Machines and Weaponry of World War I.* Machines That Won the War. New York: Gareth Stevens Pub., 2013.

Schaub, Michelle. *Vehicles of World War I.* War Vehicles. North Mankato, MN: Capstone Pub., 2014.

INTERNET SITES

FactHound offers a safe, fun way to find Internet sites related to this book. All of the sites on FactHound have been researched by our staff

Here's all you do:

Visit *www.facthound.com*

Type in this code: 9781491440957

Super-cool stuff!

Check out projects, games and lots more at
www.capstonekids.com

INDEX